Eben Norton Horsford

Sketch of the Norse Discovery of America

Eben Norton Horsford

Sketch of the Norse Discovery of America

ISBN/EAN: 9783337405113

Printed in Europe, USA, Canada, Australia, Japan

Cover: Foto ©ninafisch / pixelio.de

More available books at **www.hansebooks.com**

SKETCH

OF THE

NORSE DISCOVERY OF AMERICA

At the Festival of the Scandinavian Societies assembled

May 18, 1891, in Boston

ON THE OCCASION OF PRESENTING A TESTIMONIAL TO

EBEN NORTON HORSFORD

IN RECOGNITION OF THE FINDING OF THE LANDFALL OF LEIF ERIKSON,
THE SITE OF HIS VINELAND HOME AND OF THE ANCIENT NORSE
CITY OF NORUMBEGA, IN MASSACHUSETTS,
IN THE 43d DEGREE.

MR. HORSFORD'S RESPONSE ON RECEIVING THE TESTIMONIAL FROM MR. HENRY RANDALL IN BEHALF OF THE REPRESENTATIVES OF THE SCANDINAVIAN SOCIETIES.

I receive this beautiful gift[1] with a deep sense of the honor you bestow upon me. I regard it as an assurance to me, personally, of your good will and appreciation: but more than this, as an expression of your conviction that, in a certain sense, I have helped you to enter into possession of rights won by the enterprise and intrepidity of Northmen, nine hundred years ago.

If it be worthy of mention that what I have done has served to clear away the mists that have obscured the lustre of the great work of Rafn, I may tell you that my interest in the subject has been largely due to the influence of a Northman, Ole Bull, in whose genius and renown we all have pride ; and I may, perhaps, add that I should not have attempted a part at the unveiling of Miss Whitney's Memorial Statue, had it not been that loyalty to the memory of this friend seemed to require it of me. How largely you aided'in making that occasion memorable by your co-operation with other Scandinavians and their friends East and West— of whom I may not forget specially to mention Professor Anderson and Mrs. Ole Bull, is known to all who hear me.

For the kindred service at the unveiling of the Tablet of the Norumbega Tower, near the site of the ancient city of Norumbega, and more especially the musical features of it so gracefully and effectively supplied by the Soloist and the Choir, were a great satisfaction and pride to me.

The only return I know how to make is cordially to thank you.

I have thought it might not be unwelcome to you to hear from me, as a memento of the occasion, a few words which I conceive hold the ready and serviceable demonstration of the place of Vineland.

---

[1] An original picture in colors of Lief's house in process of building, on the bank of Charles River, at flood tide ; surmounting an inscription, followed by the names of fifty-four Scandinavian Societies, supported on one side by the figure of Lief, a copy of Miss Whitney's Statue, and on the other by an Indian Maiden with the surroundings of the New World ;— designed and executed by Mr· Philip Réiss, a Norwegian artist residing in New York ; the whole set in a broad frame of pear wood elaborately carved in illustration of the Vineland Sagas and of Scandinavian Mythology, by the Norwegian artist, Miss Amelia Strandberg, residing in Philadelphia.

SKETCH OF THE DISCOVERY OF AMERICA BY THE NORTHMEN.

It is quite in order that Scandinavians should, this year, gather in Boston, to talk of the Discovery of America by their countrymen, nine hundred years ago. It will be a pleasure, next year, to take part in celebrating the consummation of the life work of Columbus, five hundred years later.

As one, to-day, reads the Vineland Sagas, in the light of the Charts of the United States Coast Survey; in the significance of ancient New England geographical names; in the manifold contributions of the Ethnological Bureau of the Smithsonian Institution, and in the results of individual research, on the coast and in the field, he becomes aware of how greatly the range of study has been enlarged, how much the material for discussion has increased and how much has been added to the body of evidence to be considered and weighed, since the publication of the Danish Antiquaries, half a century ago.

In my address at the unveiling of the statue to Leif Erikson, four years ago, I intimated that the special fitness of the memorial, then set up in Boston, might in time become obvious. The time has come. Two years and a half ago I announced the discovery of the Landfall of Leif and of the Site of his houses in Vineland; and a year later Scandinavians united with the Council of the American Geographical Society in commemorative exercises at Watertown on the Charles, the site of the seaport of a Norwegian colony, the ancient city of Norumbega.

The name of the city was familiar to Elizabeth of England in the 16th century. It was not wholly forgotten at the time of the advent of the Puritans half a century later.

Henceforth a new interest will attach to the seat of Leif's Statue in the capital of Massachusetts. The American, native born, will come here, as of old, to rekindle his pride in his birthright. He will continue to find the spot hallowed because the great war of Independence drank deeply of inspiration from the basin of the Charles; because here Winthrop came to found a Christian Commonwealth, and because a little earlier Bradford and Standish established, a few leagues away, the Colony of the Pilgrims at Plymouth. On the shores of Massachusetts Bay, John Cabot made his landfall in 1497, and set up the emblems of sovereignty which gave to England whatever claim as against Portugal, Spain and Holland, she possessed, by right of discovery, to the soil of America.   Earlier than Cabot, the Breton French had taken possession of and occupied this region.   This was the original New France.   Here was the land of Verrazano.   It was also the land of Gomez, and the land of Cortereal.   And here came Ayllon and Miruelo. This was the earliest Baccalaos.

Not for these considerations alone is this region classic ground; but because also, it is the spot to which, centuries before, Leif and Thorfinn, the Northmen came; and because Boston Harbor was the gateway through which the founders of the first European Colony in America passed to the land of spontaneous corn and wine,—Vineland the Good.

It is now six years since I intimated in a paper on the "Landfall of John Cabot" that the name Carenas given to Cape Cod on the map of Lok had weighty import.   On this map of Lok, Carenas is linked with the name of John Cabot, the date of 1497, and the land called by Henry VII Newe-fonde-lande—a name later transferred to the great island at the mouth

Coast Survey. Map.

MASSACHUSETTS BAY

CAPE COD BAY

Blue Hills

Plymouth

Gurnet

Barnstable Harbor

Long Point

The Race
C. Arenas
Cape Cod

Highland
light

Monamoy

Cambridge

Cape Ann
(Cape Breton)

Lok's Map
1582

of the St. Lawrence. I hinted that Carenas was the heir of Kjölrnes or Kjalarnes, an Icelandic, reminiscent name, familiar in the Vineland sagas as that of a promontory where a broken ship's-keel was set up as a beacon in the sand. (See Pictorial Legend pp. 16-17.)

This hint grew out of the conviction that Kjalarnes had been evolved on successive maps into Carenas, Coaranes, C. darenes, Cape de Arenas, Cape de las Arenas, Cape Sablons, Cape Blanc, Witt Hoek, and finally, after various others, gave place to the name of Cape Cod. All these attached to the same point on our coast, the southern cape of Massachusetts Bay. The constant geographical outline, bearing a new name with every score or two of years, made the task of tracing the Landfall of Leif, through the centuries on the maps, a fascinating one. The removal, from my own mind, of every trace of doubt that the many names applied to one and the same point, has taken time.

There have come to light in the course of my researches other things of interest. Among them, besides the locality of Leif's Landfall, the site of his houses and the seat of what Rev. Dr. De Costa called the "Lost City of New England" — the ancient city of Norumbega, not the least important are the evidences of the prosecution of great industries by Northmen for a long time. Some of these discoveries such as the fisheries and the collection of maserwood led to the discovery of the site of Norumbega. They cannot fail to furnish themes of remunerative study for some time to come.

The principal result, to commemorate which the statue of Leif was set up four years ago—was the Discovery of America by Northmen. The determination of the particular island on which Leif landed, once distinct, but now joined to the mainland — at the north end of Cape Cod, and the identification of the spot on the bank of the Charles where he built his houses, illustrate the fitness of a memorial to Leif in Boston.

Of how this identification in all its details has been carried to comple-
tion, has, as I have intimated, been withheld from publication because of
my desire to leave no question in the minds of others, as to the fact of
the solution of the Problem of the Northmen.

In the brief time I may venture now to take, I can at the best give only
a summary, rather than the details, of the argument. The full presentation
of the evidence will appear at no distant day.

VINELAND.

There may be said to be two questions—one, of the existence of a Vineland, so called — a region on the west side of the Atlantic, where corn and
grapes grew without cultivation; and another question: — the latitude of
this region to which Leif, according to Icelandic history, gave the name of
Vineland.

The existence of a Vineland, at all, is generally supposed to rest
upon Icelandic records, and to share with the Vineland Sagas, whatever
criticism may befall them. This is a mistake. The question of the existence of a Vineland of corn and wine was settled in about 1070, when the
Prelate Adam of Bremen gave to the world his conversation with the
King of Denmark a few years before.

It was at the least some three hundred years later that the Vineland
sagas were written down.

In these there are substantially only four Vineland stories — Biarni's,
Leif's, Thorwald's and Thorfinn's ; and they all revolve about the Landfall
of Leif and the Site of his Houses in Vineland.

But the fact that there was a Vineland does not rest on any or all of
them. These Vineland Stories, as I have said, only reached manuscript
form, in Iceland toward the end of the fourteenth century. But Adam

of Bremen was told in a personal interview with the king of Denmark, of the *discovery* of Vineland about half a century after Thorfinn was here.

Referring to the region beyond Greenland, the king said,— *"an island, lying in that ocean, had been visited by many. It was called Vineland because grapes making excellent wine grow there spontaneously, and cereals without planting."* The king assured the Dignitary of the church that this relation was trustworthy as it came from Danes, his own subjects, who had been in Vineland.

This testimony is quite independent of the Vineland Sagas,— indeed — wholly independent of Icelandic literature. It is difficult to see what form of evidence could more surely command our confidence than the personal record, by a most scholarly, pious, enlightened and trusted officer of the Church, in a volume relating to fields of missionary labor in Northern Europe, of a conversation with the Sovereign of a Realm, whose subjects had reported to him the results of their voyages in distant seas.

It establishes the fact of a Vineland of spontaneous corn and wine in the distant western ocean; gives hints of its climate, and of its position, regarding it as an island, by itself, like Iceland.[1]

In regard to the second question as to where Vineland was, there are the Vineland Sagas.

THE VINELAND SAGAS.

They constitute a small body of Icelandic literature that has come down to us from the period of the events narrated, held for a long time in memory by frequent recitations,— the habit of the people — and as part of

[1] Adam von Bremen, Historia Eccleslastica § 246, p 151. "Preterea unam adhuc *insulam* recitavit rex Danias Suenus Estritius a multis repertam in illo Oceano, quae dicitur Winland, eo quod ibi vites sponte nascuntur vinum optimum ferentes. Nam et fruges ibi non seminatas abundare, non fabulosa opinione, sed certa Danorum comperimus relatione."

a system of education, and sometimes for professional service; transmitted
from sire and matron to son and daughter as fireside entertainment and
culture for a series of generations, and then, with the introduction of the
art of writing, transferred to parchment.

The Sagas, on which it is assumed that the old Icelandic geography —
as shown on the map of Stephanius, of the Icelandic University at
Skalholt, — and also the essential points of the earliest discovery of the
coast of New England, rest, were preserved in the families of Eirik Raude
(Erik the Red), a Norwegian of distinction, and Thorfinn Karlsefni of
Icelandic birth, a man of wealth and accredited as of royal descent.

The Vineland Sagas, in summary, if not in detail, are familiar to every
Scandinavian.

The relations of Bjarni and Leif are, obviously and thoughtfully true,
extremely simple, and free from repetition,—of the type of *"ship's logs."*

The Thorfinn relations, as given in Rafn's "Antiquitates Americanæ,"
bear witness to the difficulties that have arisen to perplex translators and
even the earliest scribes who collected and arranged the original traditions.
The forms of expression in which this feeling of doubt is conveyed on the
part of Scribes or copyists are familiar; such as " They say," or " Some
men say," or, " It is said, etc." There are, in the order of arrangement of
Thorfinn's Sagas, palpable defects of sequence, much to be criticised,
undoubtedly, if we were considering the relations as typical models of his-
torical writing ; but as a collection of recorded verities in the history of an
ancient people, to be studied not only for what is obvious, but for what
may be found between the lines, they are of inestimable value. The depar-
ture of Thorfinn's fleet from Greenland is mentioned at least *five times.*
Some of these have been mistaken for fragments of accounts of other voyages.
The relations differ in the kind and variety of minutiae which they have
preserved. In some cases, doubtless, we have hearsay. The relators may

have been on different ships, or they may not have visited the places mentioned at the same time; but closely studied, the Sagas strengthen one another,
and clear up what are obscurities to the superficial reader.

The first of them is the

STORY OF BIARNI.

Biarni, a Norwegian supercargo, who, on a voyage in 985 from Iceland
to Greenland, had been driven he knew not whither in a violent northeast
storm accompanied by fog and rain for many days, found himself as the sky
cleared, off a wooded projection of coast, without mountains, but having here
and there little hillocks in the interior.   He did not land, as the country did
not look like Greenland,— which he had heard was a region of ice-covered
mountains;—but reversed his course leaving the land on the left, and sailed
to the northeast with a fair wind, for two days; when he came to another
projection, also low, without mountains, and wooded.   Leaving this second
projection without landing, and with the same favoring wind, growing
stronger, after three days' sail, he came on a high land, and having snow-
covered mountains, which proved to be an island, the nearest part of which,
as he afterward found, was several days' sail to the southwest of Greenland.
After sailing three or four days more, under stress of canvas so great as to
compel him to shorten sail, he reached Heriulfsness, the residence of his
father, at the southern extremity of Greenland.

He had sighted the three great salients projecting into the Atlantic,
all within less than twelve days' sail southward from Greenland.   They are
given on Stephanius map—and are familiar to us on all modern maps.
They are Newfoundland, Nova Scotia and Cape Cod.

You will not fail to remark to the credit of the Sagamen and the
loyalty to the truth which they sacredly observed, that Bjarni, who has told
us so much, was not even once on shore, from the time he left Iceland till

he reached Greenland, all the way by Cape Cod, Nova Scotia, Cape Race
and Belle Isle to his father's home, at Heriulfsness.

The next story is of Leif.

LEIF'S EXPEDITION AND LANDFALL.

Leif, having heard Bjarni's story, fifteen years after his voyage, buys,
equips, and mans his ship. He first touches the land Bjarni had last discovered and coasted, notes the flat rocks along the shore and the snowy
mountains in the interior, calls it Helluland (Newfoundland) and sails away
for Bjarni's next salient, taking it in reverse. He finds the country flat, the
shore low towards the sea and sandy, lands for a little while and sails away for
the third salient. Bjarni had consumed three days from the land, low,
wooded and without mountains, (Nova Scotia) to the Island having snowy
mountains (Newfoundland).

Here is Leif's record from the time of leaving Markland, (Nova
Scotia):—

" Leif said, 'We shall give this land a name according to its kind, and
call it Markland.'   Then they hastened on board and put to sea again, with
the wind from the *northeast*, and were out for two days until they sighted
land."   Bjarni had consumed two days in sailing over the same track in the
reverse direction.   "They sailed to the country and *came to an island that
lay to the north of the mainland.*"

THIS WAS THE LANDFALL OF LEIF.

Having landed and observed the sweetness of the dew, they again em-
barked.   The Saga says,—

"Then they went on board, and *sailed across a bay* that lay between
the island and a ness that jutted out northeastward from the mainland, and
steered . . . . westward, past the ness,"—the projection.

The two great facts relating to the Landfall are— (1) *descending, in the last section of the voyage, with plain sailing from the northeast, upon an island lying to the north of the mainland; which island* (2) *and mainland had on the west, a broad bay opening out to the north.*

Let us see how much this means.

Leif sailed to the southwest from Cape Race—Newfoundland. He could not have fallen on an island on the *north* shore of Nova Scotia.

Why? First, because the north shore of Nova Scotia could not be reached from Cape Race with a *northeast wind;* and Second, if it could, Cape Breton, the Magdalen Islands, and Prince Edwards Island would have intercepted the voyage and prevented it in the time given in the Sagas by Bjarni for the voyage in the reverse direction.

Bjarni's voyage had been made from the southwest, to the southern end of Newfoundland—to Cape Race, under a strong *southwest* wind in three days.

Leif reversed the voyage with a *northeast* wind. With such a wind, which the Saga records, Leif might have reached an island against a promontory on the *southerly* shore of Nova Scotia.

The Saga relates that, after a temporary stay on the Island of the Landfall, they went on board and sailed *"through a bay,"* or *"across a bay"* (as from Cape Cod to the Gurnet), that lay between the Island and a ness that jutted out northeastward from the mainland—(as the great promontory lying between Plymouth Bay and Boston Harbor—*i. e.* from the Gurnet— Krossaness—to Nantasket). They steered the ship *westward* past the ness (as from the Gurnet past Cohasset into Boston Harbor).

That is, after leaving the Island, they sailed across a bay which opens out *northward* to the sea. It is given on Stephanius's Map.

That could not have occurred on the south side of Nova Scotia. Why? Because bays *opening out Northward* to the sea cannot occur on the *South* shore of Nova Scotia.

On reflection it will be clear, especially with the maps at hand, that this is conclusive as to the immediate region of the Landfall. It was on a coast of sand beaches, as the relations of Thorwald and Thorfinn, later, show. It could not have been on Newfoundland, since like Labrador, it has no sand-beaches. It could not have been on the coast of Maine, as there are no sand-beaches from Portland to Frenchman's Bay.[1]

Had it depended on a belt of sandy shore with wooded lowland and the absence of mountains, as these features are common to Nova Scotia and Cape Cod, the evidence would have been inadequate; but as the landfall depended on these two *combined with a third*, which *can not* be on the coast of Nova Scotia ; to wit ; a bay on the *south side, opening outward to the ocean on the north,* the landfall must have been on Cape Cod. With this conclusion, the relations of Thorwald and Thorfinn are in harmony. The Island at the north end of Cape Cod continued down to 1602—and was observed, after Leif, by Cosa in 1500, Ruysch in 1507, Allefonsce in 1543, and Gosnold in 1602. The Icelandic school map of Stephanius, used to teach the story of Vineland, and the coast survey maps support each other.

About Cape Cod still lingers the name of Vineland,— in Vineyard Sound and Martha's Vineyard. The Dutch maps of nearly three hundred years ago had, along the coast north of Cape Cod, the name Wyngaerd's Eylandt — and Wyngaerd's Hook. On a French map,[2] Vingaert's Eylan is placed directly against the name of Cambridge — an inland locality. Vingaert or Wyngaerd is Dutch for Vineland. Originally, this whole region was supposed to be made up of Islands. (Ramusio).

FROM THE LANDFALL TO THE SITE OF LEIF'S HOUSES.

Let us now accompany Leif from the Landfall to the site of his houses. We have seen that "returning to their ship, they sailed across a bay

---

[1] The two projections having sand-beaches are Nova Scotia and Cape Cod. Lief sailed southward to his Landfall from the more northern of the two.

[2] A photographic copy from an original, never published, loaned to me by the late Gen. Barlow.

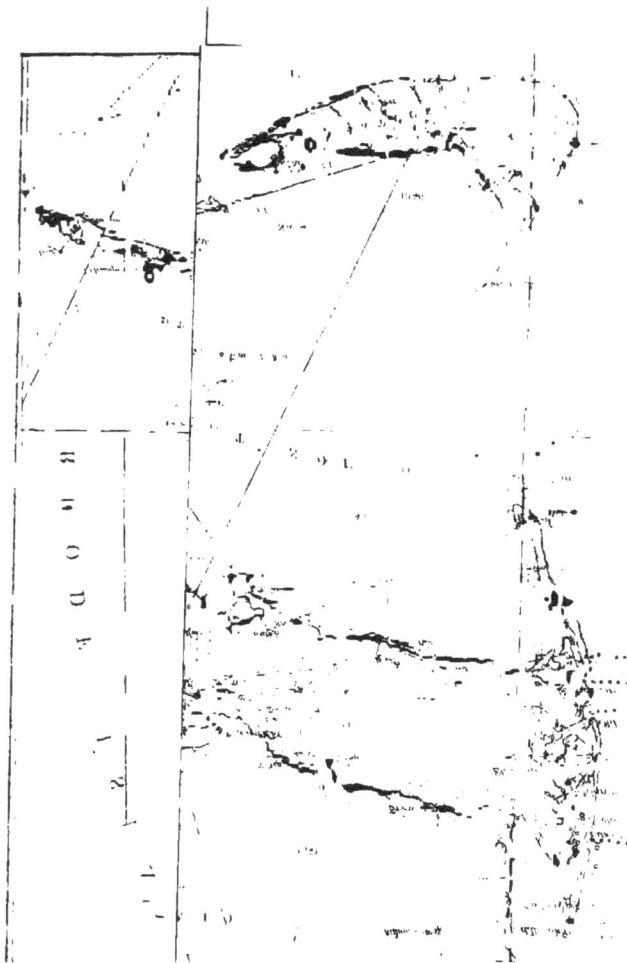

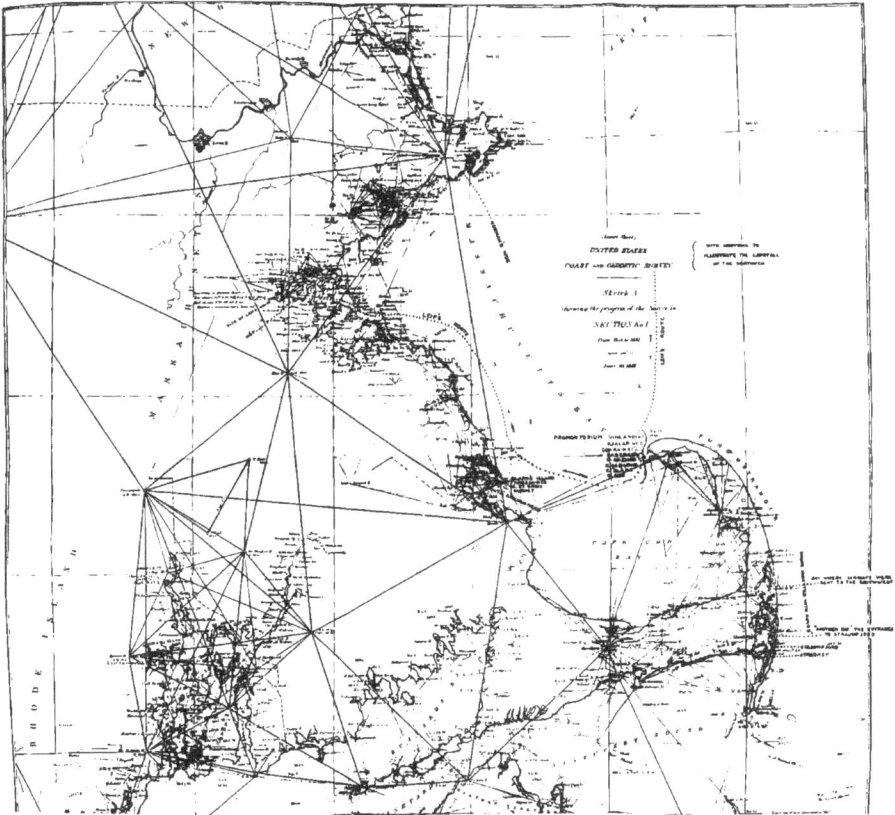

UNITED STATES
COAST and GEODETIC SURVEY

Sketch I
Showing the progress of the Survey in
SECTION No 1
From 1844 to 1868

which lay between the island and a promontory running from the mainland toward the northeast, and directing their course westward they passed beyond this promontory."

They had come across the mouth of Cape Cod Bay, past the Gurnet, and Cohasset rocks, and into Boston Bay.

Thorfinn mentions that *"before the mouth of the river were great Islands."* There are some forty large and small in Boston Harbor and at its entrance. This river flowed through the *"Hóp'—a small landlocked bay salt at flood tide and fresh at ebb"*—our ancient Boston Back Bay. There is not another "Hóp" on our coast with a bay to the southeast opening outward to the north and a promontory of sand beyond. Stephanius' map, the Coast Survey and the Admiralty Charts place this beyond question.

The Saga says, "In the bay there were great shoals at ebb-tide, and the vessel *stood up*, and it was far to see from the ship to the sea."

That is to say: *They grounded in ebb-tide, on soft bottom, against Fort Point, opposite Noddle's Island (East Boston),* as one sees on the pilot chart of Boston Harbor.

"So great was the desire of the men to go ashore, that they would not wait the return of the tide, but sprang ashore and ran to the land where a river flows out of a lake."

And this was the mouth of the river between Fort Point and East Boston.

"So soon as the waters rose up under the ship, then took they their boats and rowed to the ship, and it *moved up the river*, and thence into the lake, and there they cast anchor."

The ship *moved*, that is, *floated of itself* up the river on the *flood tide* into the lake (the ancient Boston Back Bay).

[1]Thorfinn gave this descriptive name. Leif spoke of it as a Lake through which a river flowed to the sea. The Saga also mentions that the river flowed from the west to the east.

Except at high tide the vessel (it was a merchant-ship bought of Bjarni) could not enter the Charles above the Lake (the inner mouth), that is, near and below the Brookline Bridge.   Thorfinn states this later of his vessel.

There is no practicable landing place going up the · Charles river from the entrance to the Back Bay — between Charlestown and Copp's Hill, — to Symond's Hill, near Gerry's Landing, — against the foot of Appleton Street, Cambridge.[1]   Why?   Because, on a rising tide there is *only mud* on either side of the channel throughout the Back Bay : nor could they land in the meadows above, subject as they are to overflow at high tide.

" They brought up from the ship their skin cots, and made booths. After this they took counsel together, resolved to remain for the winter, and built there large houses."

ALL WHO FOLLOWED LEIF FROM BRATTAHLID IN GREENLAND CAME TO LEIF'S HOUSES.

First, of those who came after Leif in point of time, was Thorwald.

The Saga says " Thorwald, Leif's brother, two years after Leif's return, upon consultation with Leif, made ready for his voyage, and put to sea. Nothing is said of the expedition until *they came to Leif's houses.*"

Thorfinn, with his expedition of three or more vessels and one hundred and sixty souls, of whom seven were women, came — with at least the part

---

[1] It is not necessary to remind one who has been at sea that in order conveniently to land from a plank at both high and low water, the ship should rest on an even keel — and that the practicable shore cannot be of *meadows overflowed at high tide* — but must be *solid land* clearly above the marsh level.   The Ancient Bluff of Symond's Hill was thirty-five feet above high water, and must have arrested the attention of Leif, even from the region of the Brookline bridge.   The great mass of Symond's Hill, a bank of gravel, has, within some thirty odd years, been carried away to fill the so-called present Boston Back Bay district.   Leif is conceived to have landed near the southern end of the Bluff, at Gerry's Landing, where the shore is bold and hard.

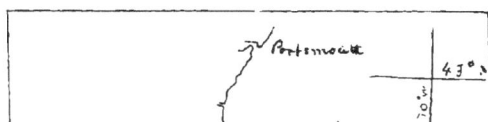

Portsmouth

43°

10°

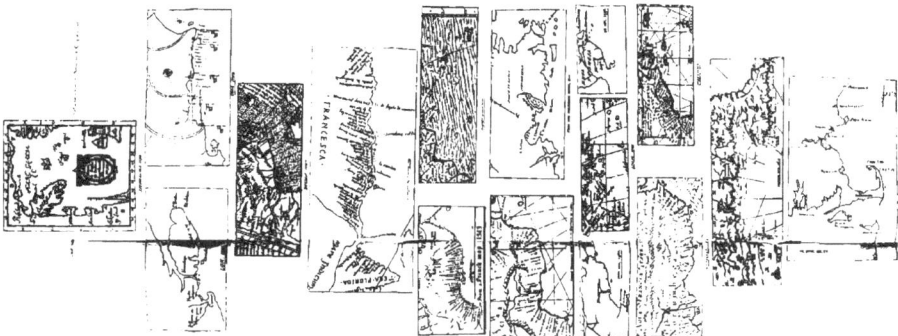

·FRANCESCA·

·LA FLORIDA·

of the fleet which contained his wife Gudrid, the women of the colony,
Bjarni Grimolfson, and the larger part of the company — *directly to Leif's
houses,* and built additional houses.

Freydis in the joint expedition with Helge and Finnbogi *came to Leif's
houses.*

What a fortunate circumstance that there were so many of Norse blood
and habits, resident, successively in the same houses! They must have
looked out on the same landscapes, fished from the same banks, rowed on the
same river, and had more or less of common experiences. Their narrations
must have some qualities in common. In a certain sense their Sagas must be
like the Gospels. They must be repetitions. The student of the Sagas
appreciates this, and it helps and guards his judgment.

All that is recorded as having been seen about the residence of Leif in
Vineland, whether by him or his brother Thorwald, or by Thorfinn or Gudrid or Freydis: — all that is said of houses, some nearer to the water and
some farther away ; — of fish pits in which the fish were taken in the spawning season ; — of salmon fishing in winter ; — of the collection of maser wood,
the canals for transporting it, and the cliff on which it was piled to dry ; —
of the points of compass, as the river flowing toward the house, from *Southeast* to *Northwest;* of the Skraelings issuing in canoes from behind the
promontory at the *South;* of the Landing by Thorfinn on his return from
seeking Thorhall, on the *Southwest bank;* of the skin-boats — the birch-
bark canoes, and of the paddles held upright as the canoes floated on the
ebb-tide ; of the barter of furs for red cloth and the products of the dairy ; — of
the collisions and the flag of truce (the white shield), — of the newly planted
corn in Vineland, and the " white ear-of-corn " [1] two months later on Cape

[1] "*Hveiti-axe.*" White ear-of-corn. Indian Corn. The grain could not have been wheat, as has
been held. Why? Because wheat was not indigenous to America, and besides, it ripens early in
summer, while grapes do not mature till *autumn,* the time when the *bunch* of grapes and the white
ear-of-corn were *together,* brought in by the "Scots" to Thorfinn.

Cod, — of grapes and their gathering, — of the topography of the Hóp — the land-locked bay, alternately salt and fresh; and of the incidents at Leif's houses: all help to make identification of the site of the houses certain. The variety and accumulation of evidence enable us to see how impossible it is to conceive of two localities and two sets of occurrences involving movements and directions, events, coincidences and sequences, —- agreeing with each other in so many particulars.

When I had predicted several years ago, at a scientific gathering, that Leif's houses once occupied a specific locality of limited extent, I had not recently been at the place, nor did I for more than a year thereafter visit it, as it had not occurred to me that the remains of wooden dwelling houses could have been so long preserved. So it happened that in finding the outlines of the foundations of houses, the fishpits, and the extraordinary combinations of topographical features required by the Sagas, as soon as I looked for them, I had the satisfaction of witnessing what might be regarded as the fulfilment of my predictions—that is, my deductions from the Vineland Sagas applied to the charts of the Coast Survey, in the light of my studies on the coast and in the field.

THORWALD AND CAPE COD.

There is a kind of evidence that appeals to some with greater force even than the argument resting on Geography and Hydrography, not necessarily because it is intrinsically superior, but because we are more familiar with it. It is the evidence of *Household utensils, of implements and decorations*, into which stone and pottery, and metals, as iron, brass, and copper, enter. Of these numerous specimens have been found in eastern Massachusetts.

There is another kind of evidence that takes still higher place. It is that of *Inscription.* - Of this type I may mention an instance. It is of a

pictorial Saga, the companion to Thorwald's story of his shipwreck on Cape
Cod. The inscription is upon a tablet of fine slate, some four inches long,

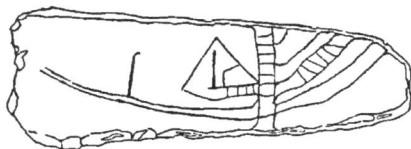

found with a human skeleton, a brass shield, and a fragment of what seemed
to be an iron sword, in a grave not far from the ancient residence of a
family known in the time of Winthrop and later, by the name of Norman,
and near the little Island given on the local maps of Essex county as Norman's Woe (Ö), on the north shore of Massachusetts Bay. It was along
this coast that Thorwald was sailing (so I divine from the Sagas) when a storm
arose which wrecked his vessel, breaking *off* *the* *keel* upon the low neck,
outside Provincetown Harbor, which connects Long Point with the Race, —
the western angle of the Island of Leif's Landfall. On this neck — the
extension of the ancient Island now joined, by drifting sands, to the mainland, near the Highland Light, — Thorwald, after repairing his ship, set up
the old Keel in the sand, and called the place *Kjalarnes*—*the* *Promontory*
of *the* *Keel*, the present Cape Cod.

This tablet, still preserved in the Museum of the Essex Institute at
Salem, may, I believe, be regarded as a pictorial record of the repair of
Thorwald's ship at the extemporized ship yard on Cape Cod, in the year
1004. It exhibits the lines of skids and other conveniences for hauling up
the vessel, to make the bottom accessible, and the old Keel set up on the
neck, so confirming the story of the renewal of the Keel, told in the Saga of
Erik the Red.

THE LATITUDE OF VINELAND.

I ask your attention to another point to which great interest attaches — the latitude of Vineland.

Leif related that "on the shortest day of the year in Vineland they had the sun at *eykt* and *dagmal*"— the afternoon lunch, and the breakfast.[1] It was equivalent to saying that on the shortest day of the year, in Vineland, the sun rose at half past seven and set at half past four. This was exceptional. It could not have been in Greenland or Iceland, as he knew, and as was generally known. It was new, in the experience of the ship's company. They had never before been so far south.[2]

It was early seen that this observation held the Key to the latitude of Vineland.

Eykt was a meal between dinner and supper, and dagmal was breakfast as distant in the forenoon from the midday meal as Eykt was in the afternoon. These times fell at sunrise and sunset in Vineland on December 21st.

As Eykt and Dagmal were points, or brief intervals of time, like sunset and sunrise, if one could know the time by the watch, when Eykt occurred at sunset on the shortest day of the year, at a given place, he would know that the length of the shortest day of the year *at that place* was *nine hours*. Knowing the length of this, the shortest day, a little calculation gives the latitude. How was this found out?

It happened once that Snorre Sturleson, the great poet and historian of Iceland, observed and left on record, that Eykt occurred at sunset, at his

[1] It was a Christian usage to "refer to the evening and the morning" rather than the "morning and the evening."

[2] Leif also observed that the days and nights were more nearly equal in Vineland than they were in Greenland or Iceland.

residence — Reykholt — on the opening day of winter—that is, on the first Saturday between the 11th and the 17th of October.

To know then, the time of Eykt, it was only necessary to know at what hour and minute sunset took place at Snorre's residence on the opening day of the Icelandic winter—about the middle of October. The enlightened King of Denmark, made aware of this, directed Thorlacius, an astronomer, to determine by careful observation the exact time of sunset on this day at Reykholt.

It was found to be at half-past four. This was the moment of Eykt. An event occurring at Eykt occurred at half-past four in the afternoon.

This four hours and a half in the afternoon before sunset, with as much more in the forenoon, after sunrise, gave the total length of the day, as nine hours, wherever sunset and eykt might be coincident in time.

It gave to Rafn, the immortal author of the Antiquitates Americanæ, the length of the shortest day as observed by Leif in Vineland. He felt that it could be trusted. It rested on the astronomical observation of Thorlacius. The length of the shortest day in Vineland gave the latitude of Leif's houses. It was, as determined by Rafn, near Newport on the shore of Narragansett Bay, in latitude 41° 24' 10".

But, somewhat unhappily for this result, it was later found that the time of the meal, called Eykt, was not everywhere the same in Norway. It varied with the latitude and the prevailing habits of the people. At Bjornsen's home in Gudbrandsdal it is the meal taken at about five. Farther south, as in Christiania, it is half an hour later; and (north of Trondhjem?), it is said by Vigfussen, to be at half-past three.

This irregularity in Norway led Professor Storm of the University of Christiania to the conclusion that Eykt, in the sense of a *point* of time, must be given up as a factor in determining the latitude of Vineland. It must be regarded, he held, as an *hour* ending at half-past four. Certain ecclesiastical ordinances of ancient Iceland seem to lend support to this view.

I have been led to another conclusion.

The fact that Snorre records the coincident occurrence of Eykt and of sunset on a given day carries in it the chief point of interest, to wit: that one of the two factors was *variable* in its time.   The other was *uniform* in its time.   Eykt at Reykholt, as *time*, was constant.   Sunset, as *time*, was variable.   Sunset is a *point*, not an hour.   It is not the same point on successive days.[1]

Why was Eykt constant?   For various reasons.   Eykt was a meal, the time of taking which was fixed, by a *human want*.   It was the settled *custom*.   The time for this meal, like the moment of midday, for obvious domestic and social reasons, such as economy of time, the keeping of appointments, the needs of cattle and sheep, herdsmen and shepherds, attendance at school, on public gatherings, farming, fishing, etc.—must be *uniform* in the same general latitude throughout considerable districts, as the convenient and successful pursuit of their principal avocations made it desirable.   Moreover it was the chief division of time in the afternoon.   A habit becomes exacting, all the more with a people who in general, are, from necessity, constantly employed, and therefore having no time to be wasted in the needless overlapping of engagements.   Habits acquired in early life are broken up with difficulty in later years.   The Rev. Dr. Henderson, the missionary to Ice-

---

[1] Could two events, either of which required at the most but a few minutes of time, be said to be *coincident*, because they happened in the same hour?   Especially could an astronomer regard them as coincident in time, when his observations fixed one of them as occurring at the moment of 4.30, when the other might have been sixty minutes earlier?   Is it reasonable to hold that when Leif said that the sun shone at eykt and dagmal, on the shortest day of the year, he meant that each consumed an hour's time?   Bjarni and Leif came some twelve day's sail south of Greenland, where we know the shortest day of the year is about nine hours long.   What was the foundation of the confidence of Rafn that in Leif's remark was held the latitude of Vinland?   Did the astronomer know the meaning of Eykt? and if he did, and it was a *whole* hour of time, why did he not say that the *end* of Eykt was at 4.30?

land, in 1813 and 1814, says the habits and customs of the people have remained unchanged for nine hundred years.

Half past four as Eykt was a period — like that of Sunset — of a few
minutes at most, for a hurried meal, as well known at Reykholt, as twelve
or midday.

The farmers, the shepherds, the fishermen, the mothers and the child-
ren in the general latitude of Reykholt a few leagues only from Reykavik,
the present capital, on the one hand, and less from Skalholt, the great
School, on the other, would all obey the same Eykt. So it came about that
when Eirik Raude gathered his ships and their crews in Breidafjord — and
departed from Schnefelsness, within the same degree of latitude as Reykholt, for Gunniborn's Island and southern Greenland, *they took with them*
the life-long habit of a lunch at half past four. As a matter of habit the
meal and the time of it were *coupled* in their minds and their wants.
They needed the lunch at half past four as distinctly as they felt the want
of the midday meal at twelve. Eykt meant half past four, as the midday
meal meant twelve.

This habit—became a second nature—a part of their organism. They
kept it up without effort. It was ingrained, and all the appointments were
originally and naturally made to meet it, in Iceland. The boy Leif when
he went with his father to Greenland had the habit formed in Iceland — the
eykt of Reykholt. He obeyed it as he grew up. When, fifteen years later,
to manhood grown, he bought Bjarni's ship and manned it with thirty-five
sailors, he found a body of men who had lived in the habit of a lunch at half
past four and *needed* it; and when they reached Vineland they all found it
natural, convenient and *necessary* to observe the time of 4:30 for Eykt, the
afternoon meal.

There was only one day in the whole year in Vineland in which there
was the minimum of daylight at the breakfast and at the afternoon meal.

This was the 21st of December.

The *inflexibility of habit* has preserved for us the time of Eykt, and with it, the length of the shortest day in Vineland.

When I had found what seemed to be the traces of Leif's houses[1] the Coast Survey records gave me the latitude of their site.

Now if this point were, as I believe, the site of Leif's houses, the length of the shortest day there, ought to have been about nine hours.

There are some considerations in the mechanism of the heavens — the Precession of Equinoxes — that cause a slight change, year by year, of the latitude of where the day is nine hours long, on the 21st of December, and in the long time that has elapsed since Leif was in Vineland, the variations, one can see, may have been considerable. This possible variation Prof. Rafn had not taken into account, and he found Vineland at Newport — about a degree farther south than I had found it.

Professor Storm, who has established, beyond controversy, the trustworthiness of the Vineland Sagas, relying mainly on the Natural History Indications — and regarding Eykt as a *whole* hour instead of the *end* of it, found Vineland to be Nova Scotia.

I had been led to the site of Leif's houses on the Charles without regard to the length of the shortest day — from the *"logs of the ships,"* alone.

It remained to apply to my determination the evidence arising from the time of Eykt as settled by the astronomical observations of Thorlacius at Reykholt.

LATITUDE OF VINELAND.

I addressed a note to Miss Pendleton, one of the Instructors in the De-

[1] Thorfinn's Sagas had helped to define the exact site of Leif's houses.

partment of Mathematics at Wellesley College, submitting this problem.

What was the length of the shortest day of the year, eight hundred and ninety years ago, in latitude forty-two degrees, twenty-two minutes?

This was very nearly the latitude of what I had found to be the site of Lief's houses.

Miss **Pendleton** made the necessary computation and gave me the result.

Its length was *nine hours, 2 m. 58 s.*[1]

This was the length of the shortest day in the year 1000, at the spot where, according to the results of my study of the "logs" of the Vineland Sagas, once stood Lief's houses in Vineland.

The observation of Lief that Eykt and Dagmal had the sun in Vineland on the shortest day of the year, gave for the length of December 21st, in the year 1000, according to the astronomical determination of Thorlacius a day of *nine hours.*

That is to say, the length of the shortest day of the year 890 years ago, at the spot pointed out by Bjarni's and Lief's logs, and Thorfinn's Sagas, as Lief's houses, and the length of the day deduced from Lief's remark that Eykt and Dagmal had the sun on the shortest day of the year in Vineland, differ from each other by less than *three minutes.*

ARGUMENT.

The points in the Vineland Sagas which determine the precise place where Leif landed, and the spot where he built his houses, may be thus summarized.

[1] Substantially the same result, taking into account the Precession of the Equinoxes, is given by Prof. Storm, from Geelmuyden of Christiania, and also by Mr. A. W. Reeve—from Capt. Phythian of the National Observatory at Washington.

1. The fact, according to Icelandic records, of a voyage of some fourteen days' sail southwestward from Greenland, by Leif Erikson, in about the year A. D. 1000, to a region where the shortest day of the year was nine hours long, where grapes and corn grow wild, and which he called Vineland: and the coincident fact of a Vineland of fruits and wine in the Western Ocean fixed by Danish records independently of Icelandic literature.

2. The fact that Leif at the end of his voyage, after two days' plain sailing to the southwestward from the sand beaches of Cape Sable (Nova Scotia—Markland),—the first beaches to be found on the route from Greenland down our coast,—landed at the north end of a long promontory (Cape Cod) having on the west a broad and deep bay opening outward to the sea in the forty-third degree.

3. The fact of the presence of physical remains, as walls, pavements, stone dams, wharves, ditches, amphitheatres, along a river flowing from the west, through "a land-locked bay, salt at flood tide and fresh at ebb," into an archipelago, all in a province called Norway on the early maps, and in the latitude of Boston.

4. The fact that this region called Norway was in the original New France (Bancroft) and included the White-man's-land—Huitra-manna-land of the Sagas,—also called White-man's land—Wampanakke, of the Indian language at the time of King Philip who was a Wampanoag, and of the Massachusetts Bay Colony, and was occupied by white men throughout great areas, according to Spanish records, a hundred years before.

5. The fact that the names of native tribes, of numerous places in the country, and of the country itself, are familiar to us in derivatives from the name of the Norse discoverer.

The results of the research I have made may thus be summed up.

1B36 ⌐ 1839

Tab. 1

General Chart
exhibiting the
DISCOVERIES of the NORTHMEN
in the
ARCTIC REGIONS of AMERICA
during the 10th, 11th, 12th, 13th, and 14th
centuries

FROM
ACCOUNTS CONTAINED IN
OLD-NORTHERN MANUSCRIPTS
BY CHARLES C. RAFN.

Published by the Royal Society of Northern Antiquaries, Copenhagen, April 16th 1837.

DACHA HAF

HUDSONS BAY

AFRICA

CONCLUSION.

There have been brought into harmony the ancient geography of the North Atlantic, as shown on Stephanius's map, with the more recent on the Admiralty charts and the work of the United States Coast Survey; the records of sailing time and the directions in which the winds blew to Bjarni and to Lief; the coast lines and topography and their distinguishing features described by one and recognized by the other; the undercurrent of details running through the Sagas of Erik the Red and Thorfinn Karlsefni, and the lesser threads of Thorwald and Thorhall. of Tyrker and Freydis, of Gudrid and Snorre Thorbrandson—all in the same strain; the story of the King of Denmark to Adam of Bremen of the Vineland of wine and cereals, and the stories of Lief and Thorfinn of the Vineland of grapes and corn; the story of Thorwald's wreck on Cape Cod and of his setting up the old keel in the sand, and the legendary tablet found in the grave across the bay; the furs of the Northmen, and of the Breton French; the fishpits and the sacred fish at the spawning season. and also at the time of young corn plants; the pavements of Stony Brook. and the fishway at Watertown— the ancient Norumbega, on maps and in records from 1520 to 1634; the maps of Champlain and Lescarbot, and the relations of Purchas; the walls, docks and wharves of an ancient seaport at the head of tidewater on the Charles, and Leif's houses, on the same river, a league below; and lastly. the length of the shortest day of the year in Vineland, in terms which reveal its latitude[1], as identical with that of the site of Leif's houses, determined from the Ship's log contained in the Saga of Erik the Red;

[1] The latitude of the mouth of the Charles at Nantasket Roads, as astronomically determined by Thevet, coincides with that given by the Coast Survey—41° 14′; and this substantially with that of Watertown, the seat of Norumbega city, a league west of the site of Leif's houses in Cambridge.

all these have been brought by research—mainly in the field—into harmony with one another, and with the conclusion that the Landfall of Leif was in the latitude of Boston, and his Vineland home in the basin of Charles River, in the State of Massachusetts.

THE NAME AMERICA.

In thus determining the validity of the claim of the Norsemen to the honor of having discovered the western continent, five hundred years earlier than Columbus, we have incidentally laid the foundation for ending some long standing misapprehension.

It has been often suggested that the name of the continent ought to have been Columbia, not America. This is natural in view of his great services. But the question is rather one of sequences than of justice.

Let us look at the dates. Cabot, Columbus, and Vespucius were all on the shores of the Western World, the Terra Firma, toward the close of the fifteenth century. John Cabot came to Cape Ann and Massachusetts Bay in 1497; Columbus was at the mouth of the Orinoco and along the coast of Venezuela in 1498; and Americus Vespucius reached the same coast with Ojeda, in 1499.[1] Before either of them the Breton French were in Massachusetts; and not improbably the Welsh, under Madoc, had been somewhere here; and earlier than they were the Northmen; and earlier still, were Christian missionaries of the order of St. Columba, who gave the name the Northmen found — "*Irland it Mikla*" = *Ireland the great;* and which was also called *Huitra-manna-land* = *White-man's land.*

[1] In the suit by heirs of Columbus against the Crown, 1508, Ojeda testified that on his voyage of 1499 (in which he landed on the coast of Venezuela), he was accompanied by "Juan de la Cosa, piloto, e morigo Vespuche, e otros pilotos." Judge Force says (Cong. des Americanistes p. 280, 1879), "*there is no other record evidence of his (Vespuche) having made a Spanish voyage.*"

Professor Marcou sustains, with Varnhagen, the claim that Vespucius was on the coast of Central America, with Pinzon and Solis, in 1497.

It may not be practicable if it be possible to justly apportion credit relatively due to priority of discovery and magnitude of service.

It would have been a nearer approach to the "fitness of things," if the "original New France" had been somewhere preserved in New England if the name of Columbus, now borne by a single State south of the Isthmus, had included the whole territory down to Terra del Fuego; and if Cabot's name instead of having been given merely to the strait separating the Island of Cape Breton from Newfoundland, had been bestowed upon the region facing Massachusetts Bay.   What has happened?

Vespucius wrote of the voyages he had made to the New World — of his having been on the coast of Terra Firma.   The name America first appeared in print in connection with the new world in 1507, five years before Vespucius died, but on maps only after his death.

How the name America came to be adopted has been consummately treated by Professor Jules Marcou.   He has established the presence of a tribe of natives, still in considerable numbers, in Central America long known as Amerriques ; and also of a range of mountains and a river having the name Amerrique.

Professor Marcou points out the eminent probability that Vespucius heard the name, when on the American coast, and observed its resemblance to Amerigo, his own Christian name.   It seems not impossible that his letters to persons in high place, giving an account of his voyages may have influenced the suggestion that the Western World should have been called America.

That Vespucius found the name on the Western Continent may not admit of question ; but whether he did or not, the name *was here*, and Columbus knew its dialectic equivalent in *Jamaica,* and possibly in other less obvious forms as early as 1494,—*five years before the voyage of Ojeda.*

What of this name ? How did it arise ?

America. Repeat the name in undertone and listen to the suggestion that arises. One may ask if the honor due to the Northmen may not have been vindicated from the very outset.

That the name *America*, is not inappropriate to the Western World, and that it perpetuates the claims of Erik as Discoverer when he landed on Greenland in 982, I have discussed at length in a paper now nearly ready for the press.

Leif succeeded to his father's possessions, and added to them Helluland, Markland, and Vineland. These accessions are recognized as *subordinate parts* of Greenland, on the ancient and authoritative map of Stephanius, used at the university of Skalholt, Iceland, to teach the story of Erik the Red.

The utterance of Norse forms of the name, as Eirikr, Æirekr, Eyrikur, suggests, to a listener, *Erika*, which needs only the prefix *m*, one of the features of speech due to imperfect vocal development, remarked among American aboriginal races, and especially among the Indian tribes of the region of Norumbega (Vineland), to become *Em-erika*, or not remotely *America*, the name which the continent, as I conceive, has appropriately borne. I say appropriately, because the Northmen seem to have spread widely over the Northern half of the Continent and much of the Southern half, leaving traces of their presence from a period long antedating the discovery by Columbus.